Ink and Grace:
Odes to My
Red-Haired Tattooed Muse

Table of Contents

Ismael S. Rodriguez Jr. 365 Northwest 43rd Court Oakland Park, FL 33309

https://thebulletproofpoet1.godaddysites.com/home

Ink and Grace: Odes to My Tattooed Muse /Ismael S. Rodriguez Jr.

Foreword

Ink and Grace: Odes to My Tattooed Muse is a collection that intertwines the realms of art, poetry, and human experience. At its heart lies a celebration of individuality, resilience, and the beauty found within the intricate lines of tattoos.

Maud Frainklen, the muse who inspired these verses, embodies a captivating blend of strength, grace, and rebellion. Her adorned skin serves as a canvas for stories—each masterpiece inked a chapter in her journey, a testament to her experiences, passions, and dreams.

In these pages, you will embark on a poetic exploration of Maud's world—a world where tattoos are not merely ink on skin, but vibrant symbols of identity, memory, and self-expression. Through the lens of poetry, we delve into the layers of meaning behind each tattoo, unraveling the narratives woven into the fabric of Maud's being.

Yet, Ink and Grace goes beyond mere admiration of body art; it delves into the essence of beauty found in imperfection, in the scars and stories that shape us. It celebrates the courage to embrace one's true self, unapologetically and authentically, just as Maud does with every tattoo she wears.

As you immerse yourself in these odes, may you find inspiration in Maud's journey—a journey marked by resilience, empowerment, and unwavering self-love. May you discover the beauty in your own stories, the poetry within your scars, and the grace that resides within every line of ink.

This collection is a tribute to Maud Frainklen, to her indomitable spirit, and to the transformative power of art and self-expression. May it serve as a reminder that within the canvas of our lives, every scar, every tattoo, is a testament to our strength, our resilience, and our capacity to find beauty in the most unexpected places.

With Ink and Grace, I invite you to join me on a journey—a journey of self-discovery, of embracing imperfections, and of celebrating the beauty of being unapologetically yourself.

Welcome to the world of Ink and Grace.

Ismael S Rodriguez Jr

Ink and Grace: A Prelude

Welcome, wanderers of word and ink,
To a world where poetry and art interlink.
In this realm where tattoos meet verse,
Let us embark on a journey diverse.
Step into the mystical land of Maud,
An alt-model, a muse, a goddess of ink broad.
Her canvas, a skin of stories untold,
Of passions, dreams, and emotions to unfold.
In every line and curve of her tattoos,
Lies a tale waiting for its poetic dues.
A symphony of symbols, a map of her soul,
Inviting the bard to explore, to cajole.
From the delicate petals of a blooming rose,
To the fierce gaze of a raven, she chose
To adorn her body with art so fine,
Each design a piece of her truth divine.
Her ink, a testament to her wild spirit,
Unapologetic, fierce, a fire lit.
In a world that craves conformity,
Maud stands tall, a beacon of authenticity.
And so, dear wanderers, let us begin,
To unravel the mysteries of her ink and skin.
With each poem, a piece of her essence we'll find,
A reflection of beauty, raw and unconfined.
Let our words dance upon her tattoos,
Paying homage to the art she boldly pursues.
From the petals to the wings, the stars to the moon,
We'll weave a tapestry of verses, a poetic boon.
For in Maud's world, ink and grace collide,
A symphony of art and words, a wild ride.

So let us dive deep, let our pens flow free,

As we explore this muse, this alt-model, this she.

Through the prism of poetry, we'll see her anew,

A kaleidoscope of colors, a spectrum of hues.

For in her tattoos, a universe resides,

Of love, of loss, of hope, and of pride.

And as we embark on this journey of ink and verse,

Let us remember the power of art to immerse.

For in Maud's story, we may find our own,

A reflection of the truths we've never shown.

So come, dear friends, let us wander and explore,

Through the landscapes of ink, forevermore.

With each stanza, a revelation, a key,

To unlock the mysteries of Maud's artistry.

In this prelude, we've but scratched the surface,

Of the wonders that await us in this poetic service.

So let us dive deeper, let our hearts open wide,

As we venture forth, with Maud as our guide.

For in the marriage of ink and grace,

We'll find a world of beauty, a sacred space.

Where art and poetry intertwine,

A testament to the muse, so divine.

So let the journey begin, let the verses flow,

As we explore the depths of Maud's ink, so bold.

With each poem, a piece of her we'll embrace,

In this epic ode to ink and grace.

Ginger Goddess

Flame-haired goddess, Maud the magnificent,
Crowned in red-gold tresses, heaven-sent.
Strands ignite with inner fire fervent,
Divine beauty to inspire, represent.
With each copper lock unfurled gracefully,
Imbued myths of ginger realms regally.
Her aurora presence felt tangibly,
Strength and power she has dealt ably.
Those crimson curls gleam bold, undaunted,
Resilience through ages old, vaunted.
Maud's mane by bards extolled, oft chanted,
Her hair-spun tales untold, enchanted.
O goddess of ginger, empowering,
Maud's legend ever-flowering, towering.
Titian crown awe-inspiring, embowering,
Mystical light transpiring, showering.
Let Maud's ginger glory shine eternal,
Her divine hair enshrines supernal.
Like phoenix plumes align diurnal,
Radiant queen benign, nocturnal.

A Cup of Enchantment

In a world of varied taste and view,
Where charm and beauty are deemed askew,
I know these qualities are subjective, it's true,
But for just one coffee, I'd sell my soul to you.
For in your presence, charisma does arise,
A mystic aura that captures hearts and eyes.
Your words enchant like melodies, gentle and true,
Oh, how I long for that coffee with you.
Like a sip of nectar, your charm does pour,
A magnetism that leaves me wanting more.
In your company, time would surely fly,
As we savor moments, under the coffee shop's sky.
I know beauty is subjective, my dear,
But your presence holds a radiance so clear.
To spend a moment, a conversation so true,
I'd gladly trade my soul, just for coffee with you.
For in that cherished meeting, I'd learn and grow,
From the wisdom you possess, it would surely show.
So let us share a cup, and our stories intertwine,
A moment of connection, rare and sublime.
Though charm, charisma, and beauty may be subjective,
I know that with you, they hold a magic directive.
So, here's my plea, my soul I'd give, it's true,
Just to have that precious coffee moment with you.

Alien Ink

In the depths of space, where stars ignite,
Maud drifts as a creature of cosmic light.
Her skin adorned with celestial ink,
Each tattoo is a tale from the universe's brink.
Her eyes aglow with the secrets of the stars,
Reflecting galaxies, Jupiter's scars.
In her presence, a sense of wonder unfurls,
As she dances through the cosmos, adorned with cosmic swirls.
Her tattoos speak of nebulae's birth,
Of constellations mapping paths on Earth.
Each line, a whisper from a distant realm,
A cosmic symphony, an otherworldly helm.
With every step, she leaves stardust in her wake,
A celestial being, no mortal could forsake.
In her presence, we're drawn to the unknown,
Lost in the beauty of her cosmic throne.
So let us gaze upon her with awe and respect,
For Maud, the alien, leaves us all bedecked.
With tattoos as ancient as the universe's song,
In her presence, we belong.

Muad Frainklen, the Muse

In realms of thought, where inspiration thrives,
A guiding light, a friend forever true,
Muad Frainklen, with hair of flames alive,
Ignites the spark of creativity anew.
Her presence, like a dawn of radiant hue,
Illuminates the path for those who seek,
To wander in the depths of art's mystique.
With insight deep and wisdom to impart,
She sees beyond the veil of mundane sight,
Her gaze, a portal to the realms of art,
Where dreams take flight and visions come to light.
In her, the artist finds a beacon bright,
A kindred spirit, muse, and confidante,
Whose guidance leads them through the creative hunt.
Her words, like music, lyrical and sweet,
Encourage and uplift the weary soul,
She knows the trials of the artist's feat,
The doubts and fears that take their heavy toll.
But with her faith unwavering and whole,
She helps them rise above the tempest's roar,
And find the strength to reach for something more.
Muad Frainklen, the flame-haired muse divine,
A constant friend through every joy and pain,
Her spirit, like a rich and robust wine,
Intoxicates the mind with fancies plain.
In her, the artist finds their own refrain,
A melody that echoes through their heart,
And sets their creativity apart.
With her beside them, they can conquer all,
The blank canvas, the empty page, the stage,

She is the wind beneath their wings' thrall,
The force that helps them break free from the cage.
Together, they embark on each new age,
Of exploration, wonder, and delight,
Muad Frainklen, the muse, forever bright.
Prince, in this world of artistry and skill,
Where inspiration is the holy grail,
Muad Frainklen, with hair of fire, will,
Forever be the muse that shall prevail.
Her friendship, like a comforting travail,
Guides artists through the labyrinth of their mind,
And helps them leave their masterpiece behind.

Tattooed Temptress

In the dim-lit room where shadows dance,
There stands a figure, a mystic trance.
Her skin adorned with inked designs,
Each telling tales of secret signs.
A temptress draped in swirling art,
Captivates all with every part.
Her gaze, a spell, it draws you near,
To whisper secrets in your ear.
With every step, a silent song,
Her presence lingers, oh so strong.
The runway's her stage, her domain,
Where hearts are caught in her refrain.
But beyond the lights, in quieter spaces,
Her allure remains, in hidden places.
A magnetism, an unseen force,
Leaving souls forever drawn, of course.
For she's more than flesh and bone,
A living canvas, her tattoos shown.
Each stroke, a story, a mystery untold,
In her embrace, one feels truly bold.
Tattooed temptress, enigma divine,
In your presence, hearts intertwine.
Leaving an imprint, an indelible mark,
In the souls of those who dare embark.
So, dance, oh muse, in your inked grace,
A siren's call, a mesmerizing chase.
For in your allure, we find our truth,
Bound by the beauty of eternal youth.

Tresses of Autumn

In the tapestry of seasons, Maud's hair unfurls,
A cascade of crimson, a dance of autumn's hues,
Each strand a leaf in the wind, a story it twirls,
A symphony of change, in amber and russet views.
As autumn leaves dance, so does her fiery mane,
In every flicker and twist, a whisper of transition,
From the embers of summer to the winter's refrain,
Her tresses paint the canvas of nature's rendition.
Like leaves ablaze with the setting sun's kiss,
Her hair glows with warmth, a flame against the chill,
In every curl and curl, a tale of reminisce,
A reminder of life's cycles, ever-changing, still.
In the amber light of dusk, her hair's hues ignite,
Echoing the golden days, now past but not forgotten,
Each strand a reminder of the fleeting delight,
Of autumn's embrace, in which beauty lies begotten.
So let us revel in the splendor of her autumn tress,
For in their fiery glory, we find nature's caress.

Words and Images

In the dance of words and images,
A symphony of sight and sound,
Maud weaves her tales with eloquence,
Where poetry and photographs are found.
In verse, her words like rivers flow,
A torrent of emotions they convey,
Painting pictures with each syllable,
In vibrant hues of night and day.
Through the lens, her vision clear,
Capturing moments, frozen in time,
Each photograph a story told,
In frames of prose, both bold and sublime.
Together, words and images unite,
In a harmony that's rare and true,
Blending beauty with raw emotion,
In a tapestry of both old and new.
For in the fusion of these two arts,
Lies the power to move and inspire,
To transport hearts to distant lands,
And set their spirits soaring higher.
So let us cherish this sacred bond,
Between words that speak and images that gleam,
For in their union, we find solace,
In Maud's mesmerizing multimedia dream.

Inked Canvas

Inked canvas, skin alive,
    Alive with stories, tales to thrive.
    Thrive in colors, bold and bright,
    Bright as stars in darkest night.
    Night falls softly, shadows dance,
    Dance across this skin, entrance.
    Entrance to a world untold,
    Untold secrets, ink unfolds.
    Unfolds like petals, delicate and free,
    Free to speak, to breathe, to be.
    Be the art, the masterpiece,
    Masterpiece of pain, of peace.
    Peace in pain, beauty in scars,
    Scars that tell of battles, stars.
    Stars that guide through life's rough seas,
    Seas of ink, of memories.
    Memories etched in every line,
    Line by line, a tale divine.
    Divine connection, body and art,
    Art that speaks that heals the heart.
    Heartbeats echo, rhythm true,
    True to self, to soul, to you.
    You are the canvas, life's design,
    Design of ink, forever mine.

Ode to the Muse

O Maud Frainklen, my flame-haired muse divine,
    Your presence ignites the spark of art in me.
    A well of inspiration, a creative mine,
    Your influence sets my imagination free.
    With hair like wildfire, dancing in the breeze,
    You embody the essence of a vibrant soul.
    Your spirit, a force that never fails to please,
    Enlivening my verses, making them whole.
    In moments of doubt, when words elude my grasp,
    Your gentle encouragement dispels the haze.
    Your faith unwavering, a comforting clasp,
    Guiding me through the labyrinth of phrases.
    Your laughter, a melody that fills the air,
    Infectious joy that permeates each line.
    In your company, the muse's gift is there,
    Elevating my craft, making it divine.
    Through countless hours of shared creative bliss,
    You've been a constant, a beacon shining bright.
    Your presence, a catalyst for all of this,
    A collection born from your inspiring light.
    Maud Frainklen, my gratitude knows no bounds,
    For the role you've played in shaping my art.
    In every stanza, your influence surrounds,
    A testament to the muse who stole my heart.
    So let this ode stand as a tribute true,
    To the flame-haired muse who sets my soul ablaze.
    Maud Frainklen, this collection is for you,
    A celebration of your inspiring ways.
    O muse divine, forever by my side,
    Your presence is an eternal source of light.

In your embrace, my creativity thrives,
Maud Frainklen, my muse, my guiding star, so bright.

Auburn Symphony

In the grand theatre of life, there she stands,
Maud, with auburn tresses like strands of strings,
Each hue a note in a symphony so grand,
In her hair, the melody of beauty rings.
Her locks, a sonnet sung by autumn's breeze,
A chorus of copper, amber, and gold,
Each strand a note in nature's harmonies,
A tapestry of hues so rich, so bold.
With each gentle sway, a melody unfolds,
A symphony of grace, a ballet in air,
In her hair, the tale of seasons told,
A dance of colors, beyond compare.
In the quiet moments, when the world slows down,
Her hair whispers secrets, a serenade profound,
A melody of life, in every shade and sound,
A symphony of auburn, in which beauty is found.
So let us listen closely to the music in her hair,
For in its gentle cadence, we find solace there.

Paws and Ink

In Maud's world, where ink and spirit intertwine,
There's a special place reserved for the divine.
Amongst her tattoos, a love story is penned,
With paws and ink, a bond that will not end.
In the quiet moments, where silence reigns supreme,
Her pets become her muses, in every waking dream.
Their playful antics, their gentle touch,
Inspire her art, they inspire so much.
With each stroke of the pen, with each dab of ink,
Maud immortalizes their love, without a single blink.
Their presence fuels her spirit, ignites her flame,
In their company, she finds solace, without any shame.
For in the world of tattoos, where stories unfold,
Her pets are her anchors, in a sea so cold.
Their loyalty unwavering, their love so true,
They remind her of the beauty in all that she'll do.
So let us celebrate this bond, so pure and true,
Between Maud and her pets, in all that they'll pursue.
For in their presence, in every single wink,
Lies the magic of companionship, in paws and ink.

Hello Maud, May Your Days Be as Wonderful as You Are

Hello Maud, a greeting filled with warmth and care,
    To you, my friend, a soul so bright and true.
    May every day be as wonderful and fair,
    As the delightful person that is you.
    Your smile, a beacon in the darkest night,
    Your laughter, music to my weary ears.
    Your presence brings a world of sheer delight,
    And chases away all doubts and fears.
    With kindness, you embrace both friend and stranger,
    Your heart, a haven for all those in need.
    In times of joy or when faced with danger,
    Your steadfast spirit is a comforting creed.
    So, here's to you, dear Maud, a toast to days,
    Filled with the wonder that's found in your ways.

Lines of Ink

In lines of ink, a tale unfolds,
Upon the canvas of her skin.
Each stroke a story, rich and bold,
A narrative of where she's been.
Intricate patterns, etched with care,
Symbols of love, of loss, of grace.
Each mark a memory, a flare,
A testament to time and space.
Across her flesh, they twist and twine,
Ink-drawn whispers, secrets told.
In every curve, a hidden sign,
A story waiting to unfold.
From wrist to shoulder, hip to thigh,
The tapestry of her life's design.
Each tattoo a chapter, by and by,
Ink and skin, forever entwined.
Yet beyond the art, beyond the ink,
Lies a beauty deeper still.
A soul that dares to stand and think,
To embrace imperfections, free of will.
So here I ponder, lines of ink,
And marvel at their silent song.
For in each mark, I start to think,
Resides the strength to carry on.
In lines of ink, I see her tale,
A story of resilience and grace.
A testament to hearts that prevail,
In the tapestry of time and space.

Controller Symphony

In the dim glow of the screen's embrace,
Maud's fingers dance, a symphony in grace.
A conductor of pixels, her controller in hand,
She orchestrates worlds with skill and command.
With every press, a crescendo of clicks,
Each button a note, each sequence a mix
Of skill and precision, she navigates the fray,
In the virtual realms, where heroes hold sway.
The joystick sways to her practiced touch,
Guiding avatars through realms that clutch
At the edges of imagination's domain,
Where dragons soar and kingdoms reign.
In the quiet of her gaming den,
Echoes the cadence of battles within.
Each jump, each dodge, a melody clear,
As Maud's mastery banishes fear.
The symphony builds, the tension intense,
As she faces foes with unwavering sense
Of purpose and poise, her resolve unshaken,
In the midst of chaos, she remains unbroken.
Yet amidst the frenzy, a moment of peace,
As victory beckons, the chaos will cease.
The controller stills, the music subsides,
In the aftermath of her triumphant strides.
For in the realm of pixels and dreams,
Maud reigns supreme, or so it seems.
Her controller, her baton, her instrument of might,
In the symphony of gaming, she conducts with delight.

The Muse in Motion

In the dance of light and shadow, she moves,
A living canvas, poetry in every pose.
Maud, the muse in motion, gracefully weaves,
Through the photographer's lens, her story unfolds.
With every arch of her back, every tilt of her head,
She paints a picture of elegance and grace.
Her tattoos tell tales of journeys untold,
Each inked line a testament to her embrace.
The click of the shutter, a fleeting breath,
Captures her essence, frozen in time.
A symphony of movement, a whisper of art,
In each frame, her beauty sublime.
The camera becomes her silent confidant,
As she bares her soul to its unblinking eye.
Together, they craft moments of magic,
Where truth and beauty harmoniously lie.
In the stillness of the photograph, she speaks,
A silent symphony of passion and power.
Maud, the muse in motion, forever alive,
In each frame, a masterpiece to devour.
For she is more than just a model,
She is the embodiment of art's devotion.
Maud, the muse in motion, eternal and free,
Her presence a timeless, boundless ocean.

Skin Stories

Ink upon the skin, a tale untold,
Each stroke, a story, a memory to behold.
Lines of ink, etched deep within,
Whispers of the past, where stories begin.
Upon this canvas, a life unfolds,
Intricate patterns, mysteries untold.
Each tattoo, a chapter, a piece of lore,
A journey mapped out, forevermore.
In the inked lines, secrets reside,
Echoes of laughter, tears that were cried.
Symbols of love, of loss, of pain,
A roadmap of the soul, etched in the grain.
Trace the contours, read between the lines,
Skin stories told in ancient designs.
Each mark a message, a silent plea,
To understand the depths of me.
So, gaze upon this tapestry, this living art,
And listen closely to the beating heart.
For in the ink upon the skin, you'll find,
The whispered echoes of the human mind.

Artistry in Rebellion

In the shadows of convention's rule,
Where whispers hush the rebellious soul,
There blooms a beauty, unrefined,
In inked defiance, art intertwined.
Upon the skin, a canvas bare,
Unveils tales of brave despair,
Each stroke a symbol, bold and free,
Defying norms, embracing decree.
For in the ink, rebellion thrives,
A silent protest in vibrant guise,
Against the chains of societal norms,
Where individuality steadfastly forms.
In every line, a story told,
Of journeys taken, of hearts bold,
Where scars of battles, won or lost,
Merge with ink, a testament embossed.
Oh, artistry in rebellion, let it reign,
In defiance of the mundane,
For in the ink, beauty finds its voice,
A chorus of defiance, a symphony of choice.
So let us celebrate this art,
This inked rebellion, this beating heart,
For in its defiance, we find our truth,
A testament to the beauty of youth.

The Digital Canvas

In realms of code and pixel light,
Where digital hues paint the night,
There, Maud's essence takes its flight,
A canvas born of ones and zeroes, bright.
Her words, like brushstrokes, dance and weave,
Across the screen, they gently cleave,
Crafting tales that make hearts believe,
In the power of dreams, they conceive.
Her images, snapshots of a soul,
Capturing moments, making them whole,
In pixels, emotions take their toll,
In each frame, a story to extol.
In this realm where bytes hold sway,
Maud's presence blossoms day by day,
Her online persona, a grand display,
Of artistry in the digital way.
For here, in this world of cyberspace,
Where boundaries blur, and hearts embrace,
Maud's spirit finds its resting place,
A beacon of creativity, an eternal grace.
So let us raise our virtual toast,
To the artist whose canvas is utmost,
In the digital realm, she's our host,
Her creations, a testament to boast.

Whiskers and Whispers

In the quiet corners of Maud's home,
    Where sunlight dances, and shadows roam,
    Whiskers twitch and tails unfurl,
    In the language of love, they softly swirl.
    Amidst the gentle purrs and playful paws,
    A bond of kinship, devoid of flaws.
    In the language of love, unspoken yet clear,
    Their presence whispers, drawing near.
    With each wagging tail and tender nudge,
    Maud finds solace, a refuge from the judge.
    In the depths of their eyes, secrets reside,
    A silent pact, forever side by side.
    Through life's twists and turns, they journey on,
    Their connection enduring, never gone.
    In the language of love, they find their way,
    Together they roam, come what may.
    So let us cherish these moments shared,
    In the language of love, beyond compare.
    For in the bond between human and friend,
    Whiskers whisper, love without end.

Digital Quest

In realms of code and pixels spun,
Maud's journey in the digital sun.
Through virtual worlds, she boldly roams,
Where dreams take flight and futures are sown.
A quest unfurls on the screen's bright glow,
Where avatars dance, and rivers flow.
In every pixel, a story untold,
As Maud's adventures begin to unfold.
Through forests deep and mountains high,
She ventures forth, beneath the sky.
In dungeons dark, she faces her fears,
With courage unmatched, she sheds no tears.
Yet in this realm of bytes and bytes,
Parallels to life ignite bright lights.
For every challenge faced in the game,
Reflects the struggles, not quite the same.
In digital quests, she finds her stride,
In each obstacle, lessons reside.
Persistence, patience, virtues learned,
As Maud's inner fire brightly burned.
The thrill of victory, the sting of defeat,
In digital realms, where foes compete.
But through it all, her spirit shines,
In every victory, every climb.
So let us journey with Maud in tow,
Through digital landscapes, where dreams do grow.
For in her quest, we find our own,
In the world of games, we're not alone.

Ink and Identity

In the depths of skin, a story unfolds,
Ink intertwines with tales untold.
Each stroke a whisper, each line a verse,
A tapestry of self, a lifelong curse.
From fingertips to collarbone,
Ink etches memories, all its own.
Symbols of love, symbols of strife,
In every tattoo, a piece of life.
Identity woven in black and blue,
Ink that speaks of trials anew.
A map of scars, a roadmap traced,
Each tattoo a journey embraced.
Through pain and pleasure, the needle's sting,
Identity forged; each marking brings.
A tapestry of selves, ever evolving,
Ink and identity, forever revolving.
In every line, a story resides,
Ink and identity, forever entwined.
Through the artistry of skin, we see,
The essence of self, set free.

The Poetry of Skin

Oh, how the canvas of our skin does speak,
In verses etched with needle and with ink.
Each line a stanza, every shade unique,
A story told, a tale to make us think.
Like poetry, tattoos bear secrets deep,
Emotions raw, laid bare for all to see.
In symbols, scenes, and words, they ever keep,
The essence of our souls, our history.
The artist's hand, a pen that writes in flesh,
Creating masterpieces, bold and true.
With every stroke, a poem comes afresh,
A work of art, forever in our view.
Some tattoos shout, while others softly whisper,
Their meanings are rich, like metaphors divine.
They are the sonnets, odes, and epics crisper,
Adorning skin, like verses line by line.
A dragon fierce, a symbol of one's strength,
A delicate rose, a nod to beauty rare.
Each image tells a story, has a length,
And depth of feeling, like a poem fair.
The pain of needle, like the pain of words,
Can heal, transform, and set our spirits free.
As ink seeps deep, our souls take flight like birds,
Expressing truths that only we can see.
And like the greatest poems ever penned,
Tattoos endure, a testament to life.
They are the verses that will never end,
A mark of joy, of sorrow, and of strife.
So let us celebrate this poetry,
Inscribed upon the parchment of our skin.

For in tattoos, as in verses wild and free,
We find the art that's rooted from within.
Oh, how the canvas of our skin does speak,
In verses etched with needle and with ink.
Each line a stanza, every shade unique,
A story told, a tale to make us think.

Embracing Imperfection

Scars and tattoos, a tapestry of life,
    Scars and tattoos, a tapestry of life.
    Imperfect beauty, a story to cherish,
    Imperfect beauty, a story to cherish.
    Scars and tattoos, a story to cherish,
    Imperfect beauty, a tapestry of life.
    Scars and tattoos, a story to cherish,
    Imperfect beauty, a tapestry of life.
    Each mark a chapter, etched in flesh and bone,
    Each mark a chapter, etched in flesh and bone.
    A testament to strength, a journey shown,
    A testament to strength, a journey shown.
    Each mark a chapter, a journey shown,
    A testament to strength, etched in flesh and bone.
    Each mark a chapter, a journey shown,
    A testament to strength, etched in flesh and bone.
    Scars and tattoos, a testament to strength,
    Imperfect beauty, each mark a chapter.
    Scars and tattoos, a journey shown,
    Imperfect beauty, etched in flesh and bone.
    Scars and tattoos, each mark a chapter,
    Imperfect beauty, a testament to strength.
    Scars and tattoos, etched in flesh and bone,
    Imperfect beauty, a journey shown.
    Embrace the flaws, the marks that make you whole,
    For in imperfection lies a unique soul.
    These scars and tattoos, a beautiful art,
    A canvas of life, a story to impart.

Unveiling Beauty

In the tapestry of human form, behold,
A canvas vast, where stories are told,
Each curve and line, a tale to unfold,
Unveiling beauty, rare and bold.
Not bound by norms or trends that confine,
But by the spirit, pure and divine,
Each scar, each blemish, a sacred sign,
Of a life lived fully, yours and mine.
For beauty lies not in flawless skin,
But in the depth of the soul within,
In every laugh line, every grin,
In every battle scar we win.
Embrace the hues of every shade,
The marks of time, where memories fade,
For in our imperfections, we find our braid,
A tapestry of beauty lovingly made.
So let us celebrate, with hearts unchained,
The uniqueness in every vein,
For true beauty, we need not feign,
In authenticity, we shall reign.

Portrait of Maud

Oh, Maud Frainklen, a vision to behold,
With hair like flames, a wild and untamed crown.
Your spirit, fierce and free, a sight so bold,
A force of nature, never to be bound.
Your eyes, a window to a soul profound,
Reflecting depths of passion, dark and sweet.
In them, a world of wonder can be found,
A realm where dreams and reality meet.
But it's the art that graces your fair skin,
The inked designs that tell your story true.
Each line, each shade, a chapter to begin,
A testament to all you've been through.
The tattoos that adorn your body fair,
They are like a tapestry of tales untold.
Each one a symbol, a meaning rare,
A glimpse into your heart, so brave and bold.
They speak of strength and courage, beauty too,
Of dreams and aspirations, yet to come.
They are a part of you, through and through,
A visual journey, a story sung.
Each tattoo, a masterpiece of art,
A painting on the canvas of your skin.
They speak of who you are, your very heart,
The essence of your being, deep within.
Oh, Maud, you are a walking work of art,
A poet's dream, a muse of pure delight.
Your presence, like a flame, ignites the spark,
Of inspiration, burning through the night.
Your laughter, like a melody so rare,
A sound that soothes the soul and eases care.

Your touch, electric, like a current's flare,
A connection that's intense and hard to bear.
In you, I find a kindred spirit true,
A soul that understands and feels so deep.
With you, I feel alive, born anew,
A love that's raw, a passion hard to keep.
Oh, Maud, my heart is yours, forever bound,
To you, my wild rose, my muse, my queen.
In you, perfection and beauty are found,
A portrait of a love that's seldom seen.

Witch's Brew

In the witch's brew, a spell is cast,
Maud emerges, enchanting and vast.
With tattoos as runes, she weaves her art,
A sorceress wielding magic from the heart.
Ink upon her skin, each line a charm,
A tapestry of spells, protecting from harm.
Her eyes alight with mystic flame,
Drawing admirers into her arcane domain.
In the cauldron's depths, her secrets lie,
A brew of dreams where spirits fly.
Her essence dances in the misty air,
A witch of power, beyond compare.
In the moonlit glade, she chants her song,
Echoes of magic, ancient and strong.
Through the forest's depths, her spirit roams,
A sorceress, casting spells in sacred groves.
In the witch's brew, Maud's essence blooms,
A potion of power, dispelling gloom.
For in her tattoos, the magic thrives,
A witch's brew where her spirit thrives.

Symbols on Skin

Behold the tales inked deep, forever told,
On canvas skin, a language seldom heard,
Where symbols reign, their meanings to unfold,
A visual voice, without a spoken word.
In every line and shade, a story stirred,
A tapestry of secrets, hopes, and dreams,
The essence of a soul forever spurred.
On Maud's fair skin, the symbols do adorn,
Each one a key to secrets she does keep,
A map of where her heart has been reborn,
A journey through the valleys, dark and steep.
The crescent moon upon her wrist does sleep,
A sign of change, of tides that ebb and flow,
A reminder that all things must transform, must weep.
The lotus bloom that rests upon her thigh,
A symbol of rebirth, of purity,
Despite the mud of life, still reaching high,
A testament to strength, to dignity.
The Om symbol, a chant of unity,
Upon her neck, a prayer to universes,

Unveiling Strength

In the quiet hours of the night,
Where shadows dance in the soft moonlight,
There lies a soul, raw and true,
Embracing vulnerability, breaking through.
With ink-stained hands and a heart laid bare,
Maud whispers secrets to the evening air,
Each word a thread in the tapestry of her truth,
Binding wounds with the gentlest of soothe.
She bares her scars, both seen and unseen,
In the sanctuary of vulnerability, she finds her serene,
For in the depths of her honesty, she discovers might,
And in her openness, she ignites a light.
Her courage echoes in the hearts of those who listen,
Their own vulnerabilities glisten,
For she shows them that strength lies not in hiding,
But in the courage to be unapologetically abiding.
In every tear shed and every flaw confessed,
Maud finds solace in her own unrest,
For she knows that in her authenticity,
Lies the essence of her truest beauty.
So let us raise our voices high,
In praise of vulnerability, let us testify,
For it is in our openness that we find our power,
And in embracing vulnerability, we bloom and flower.

Game Over, Continue?

In pixels bright and digital air,
    Maud faces trials with steadfast care.
    Yet, 'neath the glow of the screen's embrace,
    Lurks shadows of doubt, seeking to erase.
    "Game Over," it whispers, a dreaded decree,
    In gaming realms, and in life's decree.
    But Maud, undeterred, holds her head high,
    For in her spirit, determination does lie.
    In pixels lost and battles won,
    She finds the strength to carry on.
    For in each "Game Over," a lesson learned,
    A chance to rise, a page unturned.
    Failure, a teacher, harsh and true,
    But from its depths, resilience grew.
    Maud embraces setbacks with open arms,
    Finding solace in life's twists and turns.
    With each defeat, a spark ignites,
    Fueling her fire, igniting her sights.
    For in the face of adversity's call,
    Maud stands tall, refusing to fall.
    "Continue?" the screen beckons, a question posed,
    And with unwavering resolve, Maud's spirit shows.
    For in the heart of every gamer's creed,
    Lies the courage to continue, to succeed.
    So let us celebrate Maud's endless fight,
    Her perseverance shining through the darkest night.
    For in the face of every obstacle she meets,
    Maud's determination never retreats.

Symbols on Skin

Behold the tales inked deep, forever told,
On canvas skin, a language seldom heard,
Where symbols reign, their meanings to unfold,
A visual voice, without a spoken word.
In every line and shade, a story stirred,
A tapestry of secrets, hopes, and dreams,
The essence of a soul forever spurred.
On Maud's fair skin, the symbols do adorn,
Each one a key to secrets she does keep,
A map of where her heart has been reborn,
A journey through the valleys, dark and steep.
Each mark a sign, a meaning rich and deep,
A tale of growth, of change, of inner light,
A testament to truths she dares to reap.
The symbols etched upon her form divine,
Are echoes of the stories she holds dear,
Of trials faced, of triumphs, and of time,
Of love and loss, of joy and hidden fear.
Each one a chapter in her tale so clear,
A marker of the paths she's dared to roam,
A tribute to the strength that perseveres.
The symbols that adorn her tell a tale,
Of faith and hope, of wisdom hard-won,
Of courage in the face of fierce travail,
Of battles fought, of races bravely run.
Each one a beacon, guiding like the sun,
A reminder of the lessons learned and kept,
A promise to herself, a sacred bond.
The symbols that grace Maud's skin so fair,
Are more than simple pictures to the eye,

They are the keys to stories hidden there,
The echoes of her spirit's battle cry.
For every symbol has a reason why,
A purpose and a power to reveal,
A message that her heart cannot deny.
So let us read these symbols with respect,
And listen to the stories they impart,
For in their lines and hues, we may detect,
The deepest yearnings of the human heart.
These symbols are a language, a fine art,
A way to speak the truths we dare not say,
To wear our souls, our pains, our joys, our start.
Prince, in these symbols, there is much to find,
A world of meaning, etched in flesh and ink,
A tapestry of tales, forever signed,
Upon the skin, a bond that will not shrink.
So let us not judge lightly, nor dare to think,
That these are merely pictures, without a voice,
For in these symbols, Maud's spirit is forever linked.

Eternal Echoes: Legacy of Inspiration

In the quiet spaces where dreams unfold,
Echoes linger, tales once told,
A legacy woven in threads of light,
Guiding souls through the darkest night.
In the boundless expanse of the digital sea,
Maud's voice resonates, wild and free,
A beacon of truth, a flame burning bright,
Igniting hearts with its radiant light.
Her words, like whispers on the wind,
Carry hope to those who've sinned,
A symphony of courage, a melody of grace,
Echoing through time and space.
In pixels and ink, her stories unfurl,
Touching lives, each precious pearl,
A ripple in the vast ocean of time,
A testament to her spirit sublime.
For Maud's legacy is not confined,
To the confines of a single mind,
But spreads like wildfire, across the land,
A testament to the power of one hand.
So let us raise our voices high,
And sing of Maud beneath the sky,
For though she may have passed away,
Her inspiration will forever stay.
In the hearts of those who dare to dream,
Her light will shine, a constant gleam,
A legacy of love, of truth, of art,
Forever etched upon the human heart.

Tales of Rebellion

Ink defiance blooms,
Skin canvas of rebellion,
True self boldly shown.
Artistry rebels,
Against norms, against the grain,
Ink's silent protest.
Tattooed defiance,
Etched tales of bold rebellion,
Unveil true spirit.
Ink speaks defiance,
Whispers of nonconformity,
Rebellion's embrace.
Courage in the ink,
Each line a defiance song,
Boldly true, rebel.
Marks of empowerment,
Ink's rebellion sets us free,
Defiant beauty.
Tales of rebellion,
Ink's stories of defiance,
Courageous whispers.
Skin becomes canvas,
Tales of rebellion inscribed,
Nonconformity.
Ink's silent protest,
Tales of rebellion told true,
Embrace defiance.

The Beauty in the Lines

Adorned upon the canvas of the skin,
Tattoos unveil a tapestry divine,
A world of art, where beauty dwells within,
Each line is a stroke of genius, so fine.
The intricate designs, a masterpiece,
Weave tales of passion, love, and sacred lore,
A symphony of hues that never cease,
Unveiling depths that beckon us to explore.
From delicate blossoms to fierce dragons bold,
The ink's embrace caresses every curve,
A testament to stories yet untold,
Inviting us to marvel and observe.
Embrace the beauty in the lines that trace,
A living art upon the human race.

Marks of Passion

1. Inked on her skin,
   Passion's fire burns brightly,
   Desire's silent plea.
   2. Whispers of longing,
   Ink stains the canvas of flesh,
   Bodies entwined, art.
   3. Tattooed declarations,
   Each stroke a fervent promise,
   Passion etched in ink.
   4. Skin adorned with art,
   Passion's fervor painted bold,
   Desire's silent roar.
   5. Tracing inked contours,
   Lustful whispers on her skin,
   Passion's silent dance.
   6. Inked tales of love,
   Passion's secrets laid bare,
   Desire's sweet embrace.
   7. Bodies marked by fire,
   Ink ignites passion's flame,
   Desire's wild dance.
   8. Skin becomes canvas,
   Tattoos tell tales of passion,
   Desire's silent song.
   9. Inked upon her flesh,
   Passion's poetry unfolds,
   Desire's whispered tale.
   10. Artistry of ink,
   Passion's palette on display,
   Desire's vivid hues.

11. Marked by desire,
Ink tells stories of passion,
Bodies intertwined.
12. Inked symbols of love,
Passion's essence captured deep,
Desire's silent plea.

Ink and Identity

Ink etched on skin, a story to be told
   Of lives lived, loves lost, and truths to unfold
   Each mark a chapter, a tale to impart
   A canvas of secrets, forever to hold
   Through needle and ink, a journey of the heart
   In lines and shades, a tapestry is spun
   Reflecting the essence of the wearer, begun
   A declaration of self, bold and bright
   Identity forged; a battle hard-won
   Maud's skin tells her tale, in ink's pure light
   From pain to pride, the journey is clear
   Each tattoo a triumph, a conquered fear
   A map of the soul, for all to see
   Diversity celebrated, far and near
   In Maud's art, a world of identity
   Envoi:
   Princess of expression, let your true self shine
   In ink and identity, your story divine
   Embrace the power of art on skin
   Let your unique spirit forever be thine
   In Maud's tattoos, a new life begins

Beauty Beyond Conventions

In the mirror's gaze, she finds her truth,
Defiant against society's narrow view.
Maud, a vision of beauty, bold and free,
Embracing her tattoos with radiant glee.
For she refuses to conform to the norm,
Her skin a canvas, a rebellion was born.
Each inked line, a symbol of her grace,
Challenging conventions with every embrace.
In a world that seeks perfection's mask,
Maud stands tall, a radiant contrast.
Her tattoos speak of stories untold,
A testament to her courage, bravery and bold.
For beauty lies not in flawless guise,
But in the authenticity that never dies.
Maud's modeling is a beacon bright,
Guiding others to embrace their light.
She shatters barriers with every step,
A living testament to self-respect.
Her presence a reminder to us all,
That beauty lies within, beyond the call.
So let us celebrate Maud's defiance,
And honor her spirit, pure alliance.
For in her journey, we find the key,
To unlock the beauty in you and me.

Whispers of the Soul

In the silence, whispers of the soul arise
    Echoing through the canvas of her skin
    Maud's journey, etched in lines of ink
    A sacred story, a map of the divine
    Each mark a symbol, a secret to unwind
    A spiritual awakening, a truth to realize
    With every breath, she seeks to realize
    The depths of her being, where mysteries arise
    Threads of existence, intertwined and unwind
    Revealing the essence beneath her skin
    A connection to something greater, divine
    Transcribed in the language of art and ink
    In moments of contemplation, the ink
    Speaks to her, helping her to realize
    The path to enlightenment, a quest divine
    From the whispers of her soul, dreams arise
    A transformative journey, beneath the skin
    As the tapestry of life begins to unwind
    With each new tattoo, a chapter to unwind
    A spiritual odyssey, written in ink
    Maud's body, a temple adorned in skin
    Where the secrets of the universe realize
    From the depths of her being, visions arise
    Guiding her towards a purpose, sublime and divine
    In the whispers of her soul, a calling divine
    Urging her to explore, to seek and unwind
    The mysteries within, where answers arise
    Each step a revelation, each drop of ink
    A key to understanding, a truth to realize
    Etched forever, in the stories on her skin

Maud's journey, a testament written on skin
A spiritual awakening, a path divine
Through art and ink, she strives to realize
The whispers of her soul, a tale to unwind
In lines and shades, a sacred script of ink
Where the essence of her being shall arise
On skin, the whispers of her soul arise
A divine journey, etched in sacred ink
To unwind the mysteries, and truth realize

Wabi-Sabi Ink

In the tapestry of life, we find
    Threads of imperfection, beautifully entwined
    Each scar, each flaw, a story to tell
    Wabi-sabi whispers, "All is well"
    Nothing lasts, the ephemeral truth
    From birth to death, from age to youth
    Change is the only constant, the ebb and flow
    Tattoos fade and alter, yet still they glow
    Nothing is finished, an endless dance
    Every line and shade, a fleeting chance
    To capture a moment, a feeling, a thought
    In the unfinished art, a beauty is caught
    Nothing is perfect, a liberating sight
    Flaws and mistakes, in a different light
    Maud's tattoos, a testament to this fact
    Unique and authentic, each mark intact
    Wabi-sabi nurtures all that is authentic
    In the imperfect lines, a story poetic
    Embracing the journey, the ups and downs
    In Maud's tattoos, true beauty is found

Bridging Realms

In the vast expanse of cyberspace,
Where borders blur and lines erase,
Maud's content serves as a bridge,
Connecting worlds across the digital ridge.
Through her words, a tapestry unfurls,
Weaving tales of diverse cultures and pearls,
Each story a thread in the fabric of time,
Binding hearts in a universal rhyme.
From distant shores to lands unknown,
Her voice resonates, a comforting tone,
Bringing solace to those who feel alone,
And kindling empathy in the hearts of stone.
In her virtual realm, differences dissolve,
As barriers break and problems solve,
For in the realm of pixels and code,
Humanity finds its common abode.
With each click, a new connection made,
A bond formed that will never fade,
Uniting souls from every walk of life,
In a symphony of love, free from strife.
So let us celebrate this digital embrace,
And cherish the bonds that time can't erase,
For in Maud's content, we find the key,
To a world where all are truly free.

Legacy of Ink

Tattoos, a legacy etched in skin
A story told, a journey within
Each mark a memory, a truth to hold
A life engraved, a tale to unfold
In lines and shades, a world begins
Maud's art, a testament to her kin
A heritage passed, from pen to skin
In ink and blood, a bond to behold
Tattoos, a legacy etched in skin
Through time and tide, the ink will win
A lasting imprint, a soulful grin
When flesh and bone have long turned cold
The tattoos remain, a story bold
A legacy that will never dim
Tattoos, a legacy etched in skin
A story told, a journey within
In Maud's designs, a life is scrolled
A tapestry of truths untold
An echo of her spirit, therein
Each mark a memory, a truth to hold
A piece of Maud, forever consoled
In the hearts of those who knew her well
Her art, a bond that will never quell
A legacy that will never fold
A life engraved, a tale to unfold
In ink and skin, a story is sold
Maud's legacy, a work of art
Etched deep within the viewer's heart
A testament to a life well-tolled
Tattoos, a legacy etched in skin

In lines and shades, a world begins
A story told, a journey within
Each mark a memory, a truth to hold
A life engraved, a tale to unfold

A Dance of Ink and Grace

In the canvas of her skin, a masterpiece takes flight
A dance of ink and grace, a story brought to light
Each line a whispered promise, a secret to unfold
A symphony of shades, a tale forever told
Maud's body, a temple where art and soul unite
With every breath, the tattoos come alive and soar
Fluid strokes and graceful curves, a dance forevermore
In the ebb and flow of life, her ink remains a constant guide
A testament to beauty, a truth that can't be denied
The art and artist, entwined in a bond so pure
From the depths of her being, the tattoos tell her tale
A narrative of strength, a journey to prevail
In the dance of ink and grace, a world of wonder thrives
Where body and art coalesce, and beauty never dies
Maud's essence, captured in each mark, a story to unveil
In the tapestry of her skin, a legacy is born
A dance that will endure, from dusk to dawn
Each tattoo a brushstroke, a movement full of might
A celebration of the human form, a glorious sight
Maud's art, a testament to the power of the soul reborn
The ink dances on, a never-ending play
Of shadows and light, in a mesmerizing display
Her body, a canvas where stories come to life
Where pain and triumph, joy and strife
Are etched in lines and shades, forever there to stay
In the dance of ink and grace, a universal truth
That art and self are one, from birth to youth
Maud's tattoos, a mirror of her innermost desires
A reflection of her passions, her dreams, her fires
In each mark, a piece of her, forever in her roots

A dance of ink and grace, a story to behold
In the canvas of her skin, a masterpiece takes flight
Each line a whispered promise, a secret to unfold
A symphony of shades, a tale forever told
Maud's body, a temple where art and soul unite

Footprints in Ink

In the quiet corners of Maud's sanctuary,
Amidst the inked tapestry of her reality,
Lies a tale woven in fur and whiskers,
Where paw prints dance as silent whispers.
In the sanctuary of her ink-stained room,
Her pets become muses, dispelling gloom.
Their presence ignites her creative spark,
As they leave footprints on her heart, so stark.
Each meow, each bark, a melody sweet,
A symphony of love, an intimate retreat.
In their eyes, she finds solace and peace,
Their silent companionship, a cherished release.
Their playful antics, their gentle purrs,
Inspire her art, as inspiration stirs.
In their innocence, she finds her muse,
Their presence, a blessing she'll never lose.
In the quiet moments, when the world's at rest,
She finds solace in their warm, loving nest.
For in their presence, she finds her bliss,
A timeless bond, sealed with a kiss.
Footprints in ink, etched upon her soul,
A testament to love that makes her whole.
In their presence, her spirit takes flight,
Guided by the glow of their love's light.

The Tattoo Waltz

Ink
Dances gracefully
On Maud's skin canvas
Art
And soul
Intertwined, a masterpiece
Tattoos
Whisper stories
Of strength and beauty
Fluid
Lines, curves
A legacy born
Body
And art
Unite, forever entwined
Shades
And light
Play in harmony
Essence
Captured, etched
In each mark
Truth
Revealed, power
Of self-expression
Maud's
Innermost desires
Reflected, forever cherished
Ink
Dances gracefully
On Maud's skin canvas

The Language of Ink

Ink whispers
A secret dialect
On Maud's skin
Each symbol
A word in her story's tome
A life etched in art
Tattoos speak
Of memories and dreams
A language
Few can read
But to her, it's clear as day
Her truth, her essence
Shades and lines
Combine in harmony
A script of
Heart and soul
Telling tales of love and loss
Strength and resilience
Maud's canvas
A living testament
To her journey
Inked in time
A personal lexicon
Of growth and triumph
Skin becomes
A sacred manuscript
Revealing
Her spirit
Through the artful tongue of ink
A wordless memoir

Freckled Firelight

Ardent tresses, a flickering flame
    Burning bright, a beacon in the night
    Casting a warm glow upon her skin
    Dancing shadows, an intimate sight
    Effervescent locks, a fiery crown
    Freckled constellations, a starry map
    Glimmering strands, a radiant veil
    Haloed in the soft, tender light's wrap
    Illuminating moments, cherished and dear
    Joyful laughter, echoing in the air
    Kindling love's embrace, a passionate share
    Luminous warmth, a comforting cheer
    Maud's red hair, a mesmerizing sight
    Numinous beauty, a celestial delight
    Opulent waves, cascading with grace
    Passionate hues, an alluring invite
    Quickening hearts, with each gentle sway
    Radiant as the sun's first morning ray
    Scintillating strands, a hypnotic dance
    Tender affection, in each fiery glance
    Unleashing emotions, raw and untamed
    Vibrant as life's eternal flame
    Warm as a hearth on a winter's night
    Xanadu of comfort, love's purest light
    Yielding to the magic of her hair's spell
    Zealous devotion, a tale to tell

Galactic Sorcery

In the cosmic expanse where stars align,
There dwells a being of mystical design.
Maud, a hybrid of alien and witch,
Her presence a spell, her essence rich.
With skin adorned in celestial hues,
Her tattoos glow with otherworldly clues.
Each inked line a portal to distant realms,
Where magic weaves and mystery overwhelms.
She moves through galaxies with ethereal grace,
A cosmic dancer in the void's embrace.
Her eyes alight with ancient wisdom's gleam,
Reflecting the secrets of the universe's dream.
Maud's power flows from nebulae afar,
Her magic was fueled by each twinkling star.
She harnesses the energy of galaxies vast,
Weaving spells that echo through time's vast.
In her presence, mortals feel the cosmic pull,
Drawn to her aura, enchanted, full.
For Maud is more than mortal eyes can see,
A creature of magic, of boundless mystery.

Sunset Serenade

Serenade sunset, a symphony of hues
    Gold and orange, painting the evening muse
    Horizon across, glow warm a casting
    Sun setting, the as hair red Maud's
    Muse evening the painting, orange and gold
    Hues of symphony a, sunset serenade
    Casting a warm, glow across horizon
    Maud's red hair, the as setting sun
    Fleeting of beauty, the on reflect
    Hair her of waves, cascading in captured
    Moments fleeting, of beauty the
    Captured in, cascading waves of her hair
    Sun setting as, the hair red Maud's
    Horizon across glow, warm a casting
    Muse evening the painting orange and gold
    Serenade sunset, a symphony of hues

The Poetry of Pose and Ink

In the silence of studio lights, they converse,
A language unspoken, yet deeply rehearsed.
The language of pose and ink, intertwined,
Where stories are told, both subtle and defined.
With every arch of her back, every tilt of her head,
Maud speaks through her body, the words left unsaid.
Each pose a brushstroke on life's canvas vast,
A narrative unfolding, a story amassed.
Her tattoos, like chapters, adorn her skin,
Intricate designs, each with tales within.
They whisper of journeys, of loves lost and found,
Of dreams pursued and battles bravely bound.
In the language of pose and ink, they intertwine,
Her body is a tapestry, a work so divine.
Each tattoo a symbol, a mark of her past,
A roadmap of memories that forever last.
As Maud strikes a pose, her tattoos come alive,
Their voices harmonizing, as if to contrive
A symphony of stories, of joys and of strife,
Each movement, each line, a testament to life.
So let us listen closely to this conversation profound,
Between pose and ink, where stories abound.
For in their silent dialogue, we find the key,
To unlock the mysteries of Maud's identity.

Ink and Empowerment

Ink becomes more than mere pigment and skin,
It's a tale of self-love, a journey to begin.
In the swirling designs, a story unfolds,
Of a soul unafraid, of a spirit bold.
Each stroke of the needle, a step on the path,
To finding oneself, to embracing the wrath
Of society's norms, its narrow confines,
As Maud dares to break free, her spirit shines.
In the ink on her skin, there's a story to tell,
Of battles fought bravely, of demons quelled.
Each tattoo a reminder, a symbol of strength,
A testament to courage, going to any length.
Through the pain of the needle, she finds release,
In the beauty of art, in the echoes of peace.
Her body, a canvas, a reflection of soul,
A testament to the journey, to becoming whole.
With every new design, she claims her space,
In a world that would be silent, she finds her grace.
Ink and empowerment, intertwined as one,
A celebration of self brightly spun.
So let us raise our voices, let us sing,
Of Maud's journey of self-love, of everything
That tattoos represent, in their vibrant hue,
Ink and empowerment, forever true.

Unveiling Beauty

In inked lines upon her skin,
    A canvas vibrant, bold, and free,
    Maud defies the norms within,
    A beauty shaped by her decree.
    Her tattoos tell tales untold,
    Each mark a symbol, deeply true,
    A narrative of courage bold,
    Unveiling beauty, old and new.
    No porcelain perfection sought,
    In flaws and scars, she finds her grace,
    A beauty that can't be bought,
    In every line, a sacred space.
    For beauty blooms in every hue,
    In inked designs and subtle art,
    In daring to be boldly true,
    She finds the beauty in her heart.
    With every stroke, a story weaves,
    Of bravery, of strength untold,
    A beauty that the world perceives,
    In every tale her tattoos hold.
    So let us learn from Maud's embrace,
    To redefine beauty's decree,
    In every mark, a sacred place,
    Unveiling beauty, wild and free.

The Gamer's Lament

In the silence of the darkened room,
Where echoes linger and shadows loom,
Maud sits, a solitary figure,
Her spirit yearning to be triggered.
The screen, once alive with vibrant hues,
Now blank, devoid of digital cues.
The controller, once an extension of her hand,
Now rests, as if in a foreign land.
But within her heart, a fire burns bright,
A longing for the next digital fight.
For in the realm of pixels and code,
Her spirit soars, her passion bestowed.
Oh, how she craves the rush of the game,
The adrenaline rush, the thrill of acclaim.
To journey once more through worlds unknown,
Where courage is tested, and victories sown.
For Maud is not just a mere mortal being,
But a gamer, with dreams worth freeing.
So as the screen fades to black,
Her spirit persists, ready to attack.
For in the realm of pixels and code,
Her true essence, her spirit, is bestowed.
And though the controller may slip from her grasp,
Her love for gaming will forever clasp.
So let the screen fade to black,
For Maud's gaming heart will never lack.
For in the next adventure, her dreams will recapture,
As pixels dance, her spirit rises ever after.

Ink and Lace

Ink and lace, a stunning array,
    Where edgy meets delicate in a grand display.
    Upon her skin, tales etched deep,
    Intricate patterns, secrets to keep.
    Against the backdrop of lace so fine,
    Her tattoos dance, a tale divine.
    Ink and lace, a paradoxical sight,
    Where darkness and light intertwine with might.
    Each tattoo a chapter, a story told,
    In the language of symbols, brave and bold.
    Against the softness of lace's embrace,
    Maud's fierce beauty finds its place.
    Ink weaves through threads of delicate lace,
    A symphony of contrasts, a visual grace.
    For in the clash of rugged and refined,
    True beauty emerges, one of a kind.
    Ink and lace, a harmony rare,
    Where strength and vulnerability pair.
    Maud, the canvas, where stories unfold,
    In ink and lace, a beauty to behold.

Scarlet Stanzas

In the sea of darkness, a flame ignites,
Scarlet strands, ablaze in vibrant light.
Like tendrils of fire, they dance and sway,
A beacon of passion, lighting the way.
In each fiery curl, a story is spun,
A tapestry of dreams, never undone.
They whisper of courage, of fierce defiance,
And paint the world with bold vibrance.
With each toss of her fiery mane,
She sets the world ablaze, without refrain.
Her spirit unbound, her essence untamed,
In her crimson waves, creativity is named.
For in her scarlet stanzas, we find our muse,
A muse of fire, with nothing to lose.
She fuels our desires, she sparks our art,
And sets free the flames within our hearts.
So let us bask in her radiant glow,
As her crimson tresses continue to flow.
For in Maud's scarlet stanzas, we find our grace,
A blaze of passion, lighting up space.

Alternative Beauty

In a world where beauty's defined,
By standards narrow, cold, confined,
There blooms a rose, so fiercely free,
A vision of alternative beauty.
Ink adorns her canvas skin,
Each tattoo tells a tale within,
A rebellion against the norm,
A statement, bold, against the storm.
Her hair, a blaze of fiery hue,
Defiant strands, not bound by rue,
In scarlet waves, she finds her voice,
A symphony of strength, her choice.
Her eyes, they sparkle, fierce and bright,
Reflecting constellations of the night,
A universe within her gaze,
Where galaxies of dreams ablaze.
She dances to her own sweet tune,
Unfettered by the world's cocoon,
Embracing curves, both soft and bold,
In every line, a story told.
For she's the epitome of grace,
In her, true beauty finds its place,
Unbound by rules, she stands apart,
A masterpiece of soul and heart.
So let us raise a joyful cry,
To Maud, the rebel in the sky,
An emblem of unyielding love,
Alternative beauty, hand in glove.

Inked Muse

In hues of ink, she's sculpted, bold,
A canvas vibrant, stories told.
Each line a tale, each stroke a rhyme,
Her skin, a gallery, frozen time.
Her gaze, a beacon, fierce and true,
Transcends the bounds of what we knew.
For in her ink, there lies a grace,
A muse who wears her art with grace.
She dances on the edge of norms,
Defies the mold, her spirit storms.
No brush could capture half her fire,
No words could quench her wild desire.
In every tattoo, there's a tale,
A testament to strength, not frail.
She stands as muse, both fierce and free,
An epitome of artistry.
With every glance, she inspires more,
A vision worth immortal lore.
The artist's hand, the muse's form,
Inked beauty, unconventional norm.
She wears her ink like armor, bright,
A symbol of her fearless flight.
In her, the artist finds their voice,
In her, their visions truly rejoice.
So, here's to Maud, the muse divine,
Whose inked allure forever shines.
In her, we see the beauty true,
Inked muse, eternal and anew.

The Art of Contrasts

Maud, master of the art contrary,
    Defying norms, a chart unique carries.
    Conventions she subverts nary vary,
    Her style asserts, reverts customary.
    Amidst the mundane sea, iridescent,
    Her vibrant flair runs free, incandescent.
    Dull conformity she'll never represent,
    Embracing different, heaven-sent present.
    Society's mold she breaks fearlessly,
    Her spirit soars, partakes shamelessly.
    While others stick to stakes cheerlessly,
    Maud's path she undertakes dauntlessly.
    Complexities unfold, identities clash,
    As Maud stays true and bold, normality slash.
    Conventions she'll withhold, banality bash,
    Her uniqueness extolled; individuality brash.
    In Maud, beauty is found profoundly,
    Her differences abound astoundly.
    Authenticity crowned, enshrined soundly,
    Maud's contrasts renowned, refined groundly.

Beauty in the Unconventional

In realms where conformity holds sway,
 Where beauty's defined by rigid norms,
 Maud dares to tread a different way,
 Defying standards with her unique forms.
 Her modeling shatters plain uniforms,
 Embracing beauty's diversity.
 In Maud's bold style, convention deforms,
 For true allure lies in authenticity.
 Amidst a sea of sameness, Maud's display
 Of individuality transforms
 The landscape, causing heads to turn and say,
 "Behold, a beauty that breaks the norm."
 Her confidence, a refreshing storm,
 Rejects the notion of one recipe
 For grace. Maud's path invites reform,
 For true allure lies in authenticity.
 With every pose, she paves a new byway,
 Inspiring others to perform
 Beyond the boundaries, to convey
 Their genuine selves, to bravely inform
 The world that beauty's not meant to conform.
 Maud's message rings out clear and free:
 Embrace your truth, let your light shine warm,
 For true allure lies in authenticity.
 Society's narrow views, she holds at bay,
 Proving beauty thrives in myriad forms.
 Alternative grace, she does portray,
 Shattering expectations, breaking norms.
 Maud's modeling a refreshing reform,
 Celebrating beauty's diversity.

In her, a beacon for those who transform,
For true allure lies in authenticity.
Unconventional beauty, some may say,
But Maud redefines it on her terms.
Authenticity lights her way,
Inspiring all to challenge the norms.
Her self-expression, a vibrant quorum,
Rejecting limits imposed unfairly.
Maud's truth prevails, a bright decorum,
For true allure lies in authenticity.
Prince, let Maud's example be the norm,
Embracing beauty multiformity.
Let self-expression be the chloroform
For true allure lies in authenticity.

Canvas of Courage

In world where judgment reigns with critic's might,
    Stands Maud, a fearless warrior, armed with grace.
    Her body, canvas bold, a stirring sight,
    Unfolding tales of strength in every trace.
    Each mark and line, a brush stroke of her soul,
    Resilience etched in skin, a masterpiece.
    Though some may cast aspersions, play judge's role,
    Her spirit stands unyielding, never cease.
    With head held high, she faces scrutiny,
    Her courage, shield against the tempest's roar.
    In Maud, we find a model of bravery,
    A beacon shining bright forevermore.
    Her form, a testament to battles fought,
    In her, a warrior's heart, a triumph wrought.

Rebel's Canvas

1.

Ink stains on her skin,
Rebellion etched in each line,
Art defying norms.
2.
Ink blooms like roses,
On a canvas of defiance,
Beauty in rebellion.

3.

Whispers of inked tales,
On Maud's body, stories dance,
A rebel's solace.
4.
Tattoos whisper truths,
In the language of the bold,
Defiance defined.
5.
Skin, a tapestry,
Ink weaving tales of the brave,
Rebellion's beauty.
6.
Art on flesh, a dare,
In each tattoo, courage gleams,
Maud's silent protest.
7.
Ink trails like rivers,
Flowing with tales of freedom,

Maud's defiance blooms.

8.

On her skin, echoes,
Of rebellion's silent roar,
Ink speaks volumes.
9.
In the tattoo's ink,
Maud finds her voice, her strength,
A rebel's anthem.
10.
With each needle's touch,
Maud reclaims her autonomy,
In ink, she finds peace.
11.
Tattooed skin whispers,
Stories of resilience, strength,
Maud's silent protest.
12.
Ink on her canvas,
Maud paints her liberation,
A rebel's haiku.

Icon of Authenticity

Maud, beacon of truth, icon of authenticity,
  Forging her own path, lexicon identity.
  Mainstream ideals she'll shun with tenacity,
  Embracing her true run, genuine divinity.
  In the world of façades, Maud stands resolute,
  True to herself, evades trends convolute.
  While others chase charades, pursuits dissolute,
  Maud's spirit never fades, stays absolute.
  Her modeling breaks molds, shatters expectations,
  Authenticity unfolds, breeds innovations.
  Convention she withholds, favors creations,
  Her uniqueness extolled, spurns imitations.
  Maud's message rings out clear, a revelry:
  Embrace your truth sincere, unshackling reverie.
  To thine own self adhere, a mastery,
  Let authenticity steer triumphantly.
  An icon of her trade, a luminary,
  Maud's genuine unswayed, customary.
  In her, the proof conveyed, a summary:
  Embracing one's true shade, extraordinary

Sacred Skin

Upon her skin, a sacred tapestry,
Where ink and flesh entwine in harmony,
Each mark a symbol, a story to tell,
Of Maud's journey, a path she knows so well.
In every line, a truth she does compel,
A testament to her identity,
Her body, a temple where art does dwell.
For in her tattoos, her spirit runs free,
A canvas of her soul's reality.
In ancient times, the needle did begin,
To carve out myths and legends on the skin,
A ritual of passage, a sacred rite,
Where pain and beauty merged in holy sight.
The shaman's hand, guided by divine light,
Would mark the warrior, the healer, the kin,
With symbols of protection, power, might.
And so, the art of tattooing did win,
A place in history, a sacred sin.
And Maud, a modern shaman in her way,
Has claimed this ancient art, her soul to say,
Each tattoo a totem, a sacred sign,
That speaks of her essence, her design.
The raven on her shoulder, a divine
Messenger of wisdom, a guide to stay,
The lotus on her hip, a pure shrine,
Of resilience, rebirth, a bright array,
Of hope and strength, a light that does not stray.
Her skin, a living canvas, does proclaim,
The story of her life, her joy, her pain,
Each mark a chapter, a sacred verse,

That speaks of her triumphs and her curse.
The dragon on her back, a powerful force,
Of courage, of fire, of untamed reign,
The tree of life, her roots, her source,
Of connection, of growth, of nature's refrain,
A reminder that all life is but a chain.
For Maud, the act of tattooing is a prayer,
A meditation, a sacred moment where,
She communes with her gods, her higher self,
And lets the needle guide her, a divine elf.
The pain, a sacrifice, an offering of herself,
To the art, to the process, to the care,
Of creating beauty, of claiming her wealth,
Of spirit, of strength, of the truths she does bear,
Upon her sacred skin, a work so rare.
And so, I honor Maud, her sacred skin,
A testament to the power within,
Each tattoo, a symbol of her soul's might,
A work of art, a vision of delight.
For in a world where conformity is right,
Maud dares to be herself, to begin
To show the world that beauty, art, and light,
Can be found upon one's own skin,
A sacred masterpiece, a prize to win.
For in the ink that flows through Maud's skin,
Lies the power of the gods within.

Tattooed Dreams

Ink traces dreams spun,
On Maud's skin, fantasies drawn.
Imagination's song.
Reality entwined,
With fantasies ink-defined,
In Maud's tattooed dreams.
Each line, a story,
Whispers of past, future glory,
Ink mirrors desires.
Creativity's brush,
Painting dreams, without hush,
On Maud's canvas flesh.
Identity inked,
In each dream, a tale linked,
To Maud's inner self.
In tattoos, she finds,
Visions of her heart's designs,
Ink and dreams entwined.
Fantasy's embrace,
Mingles with reality's grace,
In Maud's tattooed dreams.

Siren of the Subculture

In the depths of the subculture's embrace,
Maud emerges, a siren of grace.
Her tattoos sing stories of defiance and might,
Drawing admirers into the depths of the night.
In the dim-lit alleys where rebels roam free,
Maud's presence captivates, a sight to see.
With each pose, she weaves a spell,
A muse of the underground, where secrets dwell.
Her inked skin a map of rebellion's tide,
A beacon for those who refuse to hide.
In the shadows, she dances with abandon,
A symbol of freedom, her spirit unburdened.
Through the lens, she channels the subversive beat,
Capturing the essence of the underground elite.
Her beauty transcends the mainstream's gaze,
In the subculture's heart, Maud's legacy stays.
A muse for the misfits, the rebels, the wild,
In her presence, the alternative scene is beguiled.
For she embodies the spirit of defiance and art,
A siren of the subculture, tattooed from the heart.

Ink and Intimacy

Upon her skin, a canvas bold,
Where tales untold, in ink, unfold.
Each stroke, a whisper of the soul,
Inscribed with secrets, taking toll.
In every line, a story lies,
A window to her heart's disguise.
Ink bleeds with intimacy's grace,
Revealing truths, in sacred space.
Each tattoo bears a piece of her,
A fragment of her character.
Through pain and ink, she finds release,
In vulnerability, finds peace.
Beneath the surface, emotions flow,
A river of depth, in ink's soft glow.
Each tattoo, a bond, an embrace,
A testament to vulnerability's grace.
In the silent language of her skin,
She bares her soul, lets love begin.
Ink and intimacy intertwine,
A tapestry of her design.
So let us gaze upon her art,
And feel the beating of her heart.
For in her tattoos, we find the key,
To understanding Maud's intimacy.

Ink and Stardust

In the vast expanse of the cosmos above,
Maud's tattoos gleam like stars of love.
Each etching upon her skin, a tale to tell,
A cosmic dance in the human shell.
Amidst the pages of this poetic soiree,
We pause to ponder her celestial array.
Ink intertwines with the universe's lore,
As Maud's journey unfolds, evermore.
Her body a canvas, a boundless space,
Where galaxies swirl and planets embrace.
Ink and stardust blend in a cosmic rhyme,
Capturing the essence of space and time.
With each tattoo, a constellation forms,
A map of her dreams in the cosmic storms.
The Milky Way weaves through her veins,
Infinite stories etched in celestial reigns.
In the heart of the collection, we find,
Maud's universe, vast and kind.
Ink and stardust, a divine duet,
Where poetry and cosmos softly met.
Through her tattoos, she reaches the stars,
And in their glow, she finds her memoirs.
Ink and stardust, an eternal bond,
In Maud's cosmic tale, we respond.
As we journey through this cosmic verse,
We're reminded of the universe's curse,
To ponder our place in the grand design,
And find solace in the stars that shine.
So let us marvel at Maud's inked art,
A testament to the human heart.

Ink and stardust, forever entwined,
In her celestial journey, we find.

Legacy of Ink and Grace

In the tapestry of time, her presence remains,
Maud's legacy endures, casting lasting chains.
Her inked verses speak, a timeless embrace,
A legacy of Ink and Grace, leaving hearts to race.
Through the years, her spirit still sings,
In the echoes of rebellion, her presence clings.
Inspiring souls to dare, to dream, to create,
In the beauty of her ink, we find our fate.
With each stroke of the pen, with each tattooed line,
Her essence lives on, a beacon divine.
For in her inked verses, we find solace and light,
Guiding us through darkness, igniting our fight.
In the hearts of the dreamers, her legacy thrives,
A testament to courage, where freedom survives.
For her inked words echo, a symphony of grace,
Celebrating the beauty in every scarred space.
So let us raise our voices, let us sing her praise,
For Maud's legacy lives on in countless ways.
In the enduring impact of her ink and her grace,
We find inspiration, in every embrace.

Beyond the Canvas

Beyond the canvas, where ink and skin meet,
    Lies the essence of Maud, a legacy complete.
    Beyond the tattoos, beyond the art's embrace,
    Her spirit roams free, leaving a lasting trace.
    In the hearts of those who felt her rebel's call,
    Maud's presence lingers, standing tall.
    Her defiance echoes in the corridors of time,
    A beacon for those seeking truth in rhyme.
    Beyond the canvas, her influence extends,
    Touching souls, inspiring new trends.
    In every act of rebellion, every stroke of art,
    Maud's spirit whispers, playing its part.
    Though her physical form may fade away,
    Her essence endures, forever to stay.
    In the hearts of those she touched, her flame still burns,
    A muse for the ages, in each soul, she yearns.
    So let us raise our voices in homage and praise,
    To Maud, whose legacy continues to blaze.
    Beyond the canvas, her spirit remains,
    In the rebel's heart, where freedom reigns.

Legacy of Ink

In the inked lines of memory's embrace,
Maud's legacy, a muse's grace.
Each tattoo a chapter, a story to tell,
In the gallery of rebels, where her influence dwells.
Her presence, a beacon in the sea of art,
Inspiring creators to pour out their heart.
In the strokes of the brush, in the poet's verse,
Maud's spirit lives on, an eternal curse.
Through the lens of time, her influence spreads wide,
A ripple effect felt far and wide.
In the tapestry of culture, her mark remains,
A testament to defiance, where rebellion reigns.
For in her ink, a revolution is found,
A legacy of courage, profound.
She paved the way for self-expression's fire,
Igniting the souls of those who aspire.
So let us raise our voices in tribute and praise,
To Maud, whose legacy never decays.
For her inked canvas continues to inspire,
A testament to her enduring fire.

Farewell to the Muse

Farewell to the Muse, a sonnet's sweet lament,
　　For Maud, the inspiration heaven-sent.
　　Her presence, like a flame that burned so bright,
　　Illuminating verses in the night.
　　In ink and grace, she cast her daring spell,
　　A siren's call that poets knew so well.
　　With every line, her essence did imbue,
　　A touch of magic, forever true.
　　But now, alas, the time has come to part,
　　To bid adieu to she who stirred the heart.
　　Though words may fade, her memory will endure,
　　A muse eternal, forever to allure.
　　So here's to Maud, a final thrill and sigh,
　　In gratitude, we bid a sweet goodbye.

Ink and Grace: A Final Ode

O Maud, my muse, my guiding light,
    Your essence, a beacon in the night.
    A force that stirred my dormant soul,
    And made my shattered pieces whole.
    From the moment I first beheld your grace,
    My world transformed, a brand new place.
    Your beauty, a symphony of art,
    That played upon my poet's heart.
    In you, I found a well of inspiration deep,
    A reason to rise from my creative sleep.
    Your spirit, a flame that ignited my pen,
    And brought to life the verses within.
    Through countless hours, I wrote and toiled,
    My ink, the medium in which I roiled.
    Each line, a tribute to your divine grace,
    Each stanza, a reflection of your radiant face.
    You were the subject of my every rhyme,
    The reason I dared to reach the sublime.
    Your presence, a constant in my mind,
    A treasure that I was blessed to find.
    And as our connection grew and thrived,
    My verses took on a life, revived.
    Inspired by your essence, your very being,
    My poetry soared, my soul agreeing.
    But it was not just in words that I expressed,
    The depth of my love, the way I was blessed.
    For ink on skin, I also did impart,
    A permanent testament to my muse's art.
    Each tattoo, a chapter in our story,
    A symbol of your grace, your glory.

From delicate flowers to soaring doves,
Each mark, a sign of my undying love.
You were the canvas upon which I drew,
The inspiration for every tattoo.
A living masterpiece, a work of art,
Forever etched upon my muse's heart.
Through joy and sorrow, laughter and tears,
We navigated life's tumultuous years.
But always, you were there, my constant guide,
A light that shone, a star by my side.
And now, as I pen this final ode,
My heart, with gratitude, overflows.
For you, my Maud, my beloved muse,
Were the reason I dared to dream, to choose.
To follow the path of the poet's call,
To bare my soul, to give my all.
You were the catalyst, the spark that ignited,
The passion within me, the fire reunited.
So let this ode stand as a testament true,
To the love and inspiration, I found in you.
A love that transcended the boundaries of time,
A bond that was forged in ink and rhyme.
For in every verse, in every line,
Your essence will forever shine.
A reminder of the muse that set me free,
And helped me become the best version of me.
Though the years may pass, and life may change,
The impact you had will never estrange.
For you, my Maud, will always be,
The muse that inspired me to see.
The beauty in the world, the magic in the air,
The power of words, the art we share.

You taught me to embrace the journey of life,
To find the grace amidst the strife.
And so, I thank you, from the depths of my heart,
For being the muse that set me apart.
For igniting the passion, the drive to create,
For being the reason, I dared to be great.
As I close this final stanza, this ode to you,
Know that my love and gratitude, forever rings true.
For in the tapestry of my life, you'll always be,
The golden thread, the masterpiece, the key.
The key to unlocking my true potential,
The muse that made my journey essential.
For without you, I would not be,
The poet, the artist, the best of me.
So farewell, my Maud, my shining star,
Know that my love for you will never be far.
In every verse, in every rhyme,
You will live on, forever sublime.
A part of me, a part of my art,
Forever etched in ink, forever in my heart.
For in the legacy of the muse and bard,
Our story will forever be unmarred.
A testament to the power of inspiration,
A love that defied all explanation.
So let the world remember our tale,
Of a muse and a poet, united without fail.
Through ink and grace, through love and art,
Two souls entwined, never to part.
For in the annals of history, we'll always be,
The embodiment of passion, of creativity.
Maud and her bard, forever and always,
Bound by the ink, the grace, the love that stays.

A reminder to all, of the power within,
When a muse and a poet together begin.
To create a world, a vision anew,
Through verses and ink, forever true.
So let our story, our legacy, endure,
A testament to the love, the art, the allure.
Of a muse and a poet, forever entwined,
In the pages of history, forever enshrined.
Farewell, my Maud, my eternal flame,
In ink and grace, forever you'll reign.

Afterword:

As I conclude this journey through the pages of "Ink and Grace: Odes to My Tattooed Muse," I find myself reflecting on the profound connection between art, poetry, and the human experience. Maud Frainklen, my muse and inspiration for this collection, has illuminated the beauty of self-expression through her adorned skin, her captivating spirit, and her unapologetic authenticity.

Throughout these verses, I've attempted to capture not only the intricate details of Maud's tattoos but also the essence of her being. Each poem serves as a testament to the power of storytelling, the resilience of the human spirit, and the transformative nature of art.

In the world of tattoos, every inked line tells a story—a narrative of love, loss, triumph, and perseverance. As we trace the contours of Maud's tattoos, we uncover layers of meaning, each marking a moment in her journey. Through these odes, I hope to honor not only Maud but also the countless individuals who find solace, strength, and empowerment in the art adorning their skin.

Beyond the physicality of tattoos lies a deeper truth—the truth of our shared humanity. In celebrating Maud's ink, we celebrate the beauty of imperfection, the courage to embrace our scars, and the freedom to express ourselves authentically, boldly, and unapologetically.

I extend my deepest gratitude to Maud Frainklen for allowing me to embark on this creative journey, for inspiring me with her grace and her ink, and for reminding me of the profound connection between art and the human soul. May these poems serve as a testament to her legacy—a legacy of ink and grace that transcends boundaries, defies conventions, and inspires us to embrace our own stories with courage, compassion, and authenticity. To delve deeper into Maud Frainklen's endeavors, explore her LinkTree: https://linktr.ee/ MaudFrainklen?utm_source=linktree_profile_share

With heartfelt gratitude,
Ismael S Rodriguez Jr

Ismael S. Rodriguez Jr., also known as The Bulletproof Poet, is a talented and diverse artist, author, and poet of Puerto Rican and Filipino descent. He was born and raised in Philadelphia, PA, and now lives in Oakland Park, FL. Rodriguez has a range of interests and experiences, including serving in the U.S. Navy and being deployed during Desert Storm. Despite facing numerous challenges in his life, including schizophrenia, PTSD, substance abuse, and homelessness, Ismael has overcome these obstacles and has been sober for 16 years. He is also actively seeking treatment for his mental and emotional health issues. In addition to his artistic pursuits, Rodriguez is an ordained reverend and practices Grey Witchcraft, Discordianism, and ceremonial magic. His website, https://thebulletproofpoet1.godaddysites.com/home, showcases his poetry, short stories, origami, and more. You can find additional links to his work on his Linktree https://linktr.ee/bulletproofpoet